THE POWER OF LOVE & FEAR:

THE POWER OF 42

THE THREE PARTS OF LOVE

At a young age I learned the value of love. Not by its abundance but in its absence. Its quite something that we don't know the value of most things unless it is the something that we have the least of. In my early life I summarized that in order to love you must do three things first.

These three things are: **Gracious**, like when someone gives you a gift at your birthday. **Merciful**, when you don't go to jail for stealing candy. **Glorious**, when you work hard for something, like doing your chores all week and then you get your allowance to go out with your friends on the weekend.

Further on in life I also learned that Love is an action, so too is being Gracious, Merciful, and Glorious. So I studied what it was to commit an action. Through my research and defined by my perspective, from my view psychology says an action can be committed only when the one who seeks to commit the action has these three things: means, motive, and opportunity. In simple terms, which I've come up with, is Availability, Willingness, and Obedience.

Availability (means)

For example, before a person can pick up a pencil from the ground, firstly, they will have to be physically able to pick up the pencil. It's unrealistic to ask a paraplegic as well as a person holding a bag of groceries in each arm to pick up a pencil off the ground.

Willingness (motive)

Secondly, the person must be willing to pick up the pencil. If the pencil is broken or has fallen into a heap of manure it is easily understood why someone might not be inclined to be willing to pick up the pencil.

Obedience (opportunity)

Lastly, the person must be obedient. You may say well if they are physically capable of picking up the pencil and lack a reason why not to pick up the pencil then they would just pick the pencil up. However, to be obedient they must understand the reason and agree with it before they will do so. Only after they understand and agree will they choose to do so and then commit the act of picking up the pencil.

Conclusion

So if we put everything so far together you can only Love, to its fullest extent, someone if you have the "means" (available to be gracious), "motive" (willingness to be merciful), and "opportunity" (obedient to be glorious), before they can choose and commit to do so.

SIX ASPECTS OF HUMANS

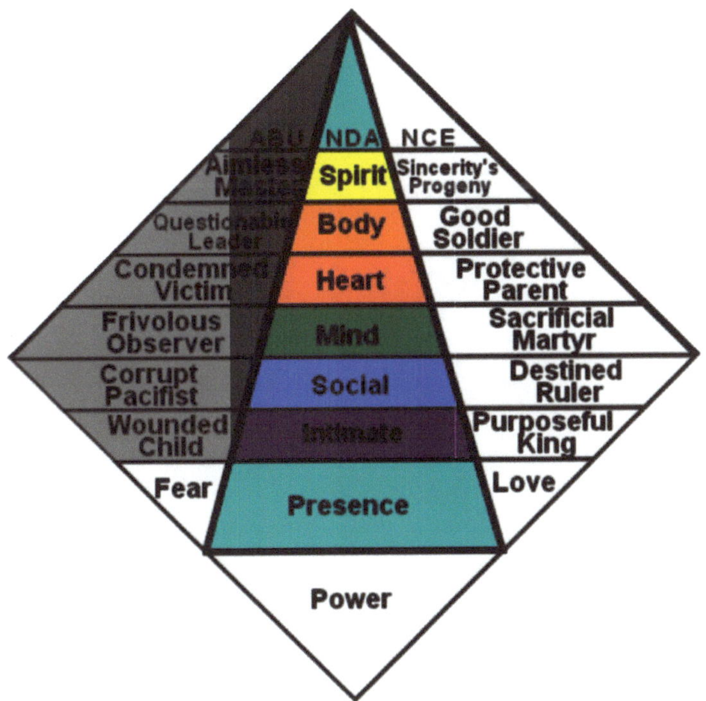

It wasn't until my early adult years did I realize that there are monumental differences about when you should love and to whom you should love. When addressing love in the limitless situational circumstances one can get quite confused in understanding that love can be good in one situation and bad in another. Like smoking in a bar is okay but smoking in someone's house could be very bad. This lead me to study to find how many situations can a human be in.

I've categorized every situation into 6 categories in this specific order. Spiritual, Physical, Emotional, Mental, Social, and Intimate. I came up with this order in which I have perceived it in the birth and development of all humans.

Spiritual Aspect

Firstly, at conception there is a metaphysical reaction that begins the transformation process turning a human from a spiritual being into a physical one.

Physical Aspect

At birth, the completion of transforming a spiritual being into a physical one.

Emotional Aspect

Upon exiting the womb, we are confronted with the pains of the needs in the world being cold and hungry which then we release this painful experience by expressing ourselves through an emotional act, we cry.

Mental Aspect

Then around two our mental capacity progresses into a state of learning more of who we are and what we as an individual want.

Social Aspect

As we develop mentally we learn that we are able to communicate, cooperate, and conflict with others outside of ourselves.

Intimate Aspect

Then, during puberty, we are awakened to the side of ourselves that desires for meaning, purpose, and closeness to others, along with the birth of the concept of thinking corporately.

Power of Love

The next thing is to discuss the Power of Love. That's right, Love has unbelievable power! Love has so much power that when used correctly it has and continues to change the course of time!

How does Love obtain it's power? Through us and our choices. This process becomes possible as we put into practice the understanding that was presented in the first chapter.

As the chapter picture depicts, Power is the sum total of **Presence** and **Abundance** when they are combined. The best analogy of this is water.

A glass of water that is splashed on you is pretty powerless. If I push you into a pool, it only results in amusement as long as you are capable of swimming. However, if I were to drop you off in the middle of the ocean with only your swim suit, that situation becomes life threatening no matter what shape you are in or what preparations you have!

Even a teaspoon of water has been proven to be powerful enough to be deadly! The measurement of Power of an element in any situation is always based on the value it has in comparison to all the other factors in its environment.
To summarize, Love is as powerful as we make it. If we choose to have Love be present in our lives and choose Love to be more abundant in our lives then any other singular factor, then Love will inevitably become the most powerful element in our environment.

OBEDIENCE: GLORIOUS VS DESTRUCTION

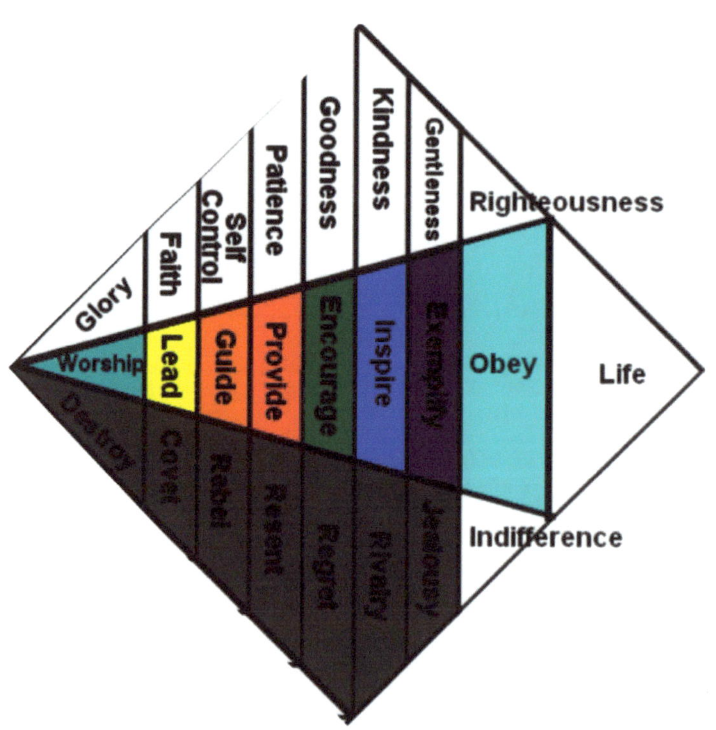

Now that we know how Love can be powerful, the next question is how will we know when have we reached a life of love?

Before we can reach our destination we have to know what our destination is. If we don't know our destination then we will never know when we have arrived to our destination. That means we could never make it to our destination or walk right on past it not even realizing we could have stopped!

So what does "living a life with the power of love" look like? Without over exaggerating or over promising reality, life in the power of love is Glorious!

As you can see in the diagram "Glorious Life of Love" there are six beautiful realities that are obtainable through the power of love.

It Extends Our Reach to…

-A perfectly balanced Faithful Spiritual Life when it's Lead by Glory's Righteousness.

-A perfectly balanced Self-Controlled Physical Life when it's Guided by Glory's Righteousness.

-A perfectly balanced Patient Emotional Life when it's Provided by Glory's Righteousness.

-A perfectly balanced Good Mental Life when it's Encouraged by Glory's Righteousness.

-A perfectly balanced Kind Social Life when it's Inspired by Glory's Righteousness.

-A perfectly balanced Gentle Intimate Life when it's Exemplified by Glory's Righteousness.

As you can see, if a person was capable of living a life described as the one above, then that one would be living quite a glorious life compared to anyone's standards. Anyone who did fulfill and live up to those expectations would indeed be considered Righteous in everyone's perspective.

If all we have to do is increase the presence of Love so abundantly that it outweighs all the other factors in the situation then why hasn't many made it?

To answer that, we have to consider what the reality of life on other side of the diagram looks like.

It Limits Our Reach to...

-A shifting Covetous Spiritual Life when it's Lead by Calamity's Indifference.

-A shifting Rebellious Physical Life when it's Guided by Calamity's Indifference.

-A shifting Resentful Emotional Life when it's Provided by Calamity's Indifference.

-A shifting Regretful Mental Life when it's Encouraged by Calamity's Indifference.

-A shifting Rivalrous Social Life when it's Inspired by Calamity's Indifference.

-A shifting Jealous Intimate Life when it's Inspired by Calamity's Indifference.

Here is where the plot thickens! Both realities for our lives are well within our grasps. As you can plainly see all you have to do is either Obey Glory's standards for Righteousness for Love and you'll be well on your way to a Glorious life. Comparatively, you can Obey Calamity's standards for Indifference for Love and live a life of chaotic destruction.

The power of making either of these outcomes a reality solely depends on which path you choose. Either worship Glory by obeying it's standards for Righteousness or worship Indifference by obeying it's standard, however it's not just that simple.

If you remember from chapter one, you cannot Obey unless first you are Available and Willing.

"What you WORSHIP will unite with you!"

WILLFULLY PRAISE: MERCY VS DEATH

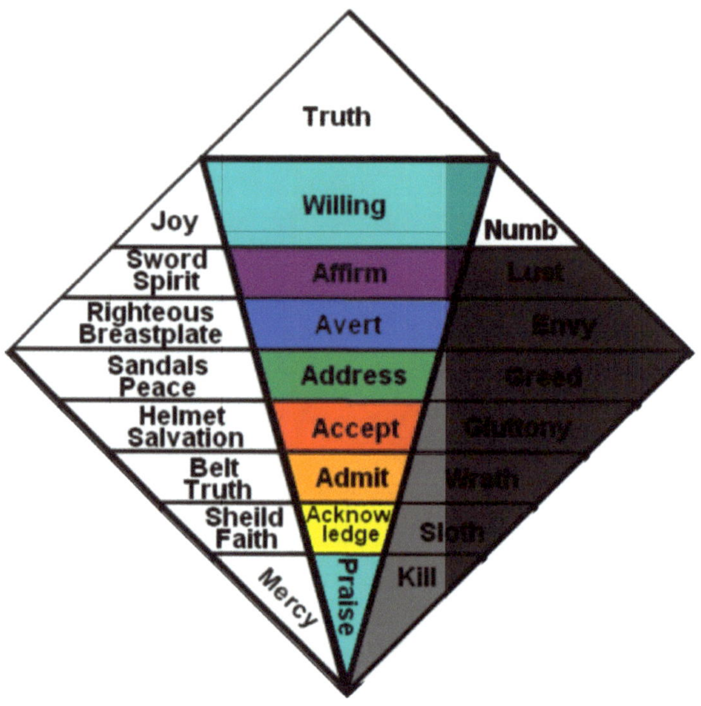

Now that we know what the destination looks like, let's see what it takes to be a Willing sojourner looks like.

Most think of life as a journey down a long never ending highway. I'm not here to say that they are wrong in the concept, but I would like to add that it is definitely not a cake walk down said highway! I would consider it more of a war path that one must endure and survive in order to find the end.

Just as any good warrior, they are fully equipped with such items to do just that. So here is an equipment list that you will need to have and use if reaching a Glorious Life of Love is your goal.

It Grants Us…

-A steady Spiritual Shield of Faith that Acknowledges Truth through Mercy's Joy.

-A steady Physical Belt of Truth that Admits Truth through Mercy's Joy.

-A steady Emotional Helmet of Salvation that Accepts Truth through Mercy's Joy.

-A steady Mental Sandals of Peace that Addresses Truth through Mercy's Joy.

-A steady Social Righteous Breastplate that Averts Lies through Mercy's Joy.

-A steady Intimate Spiritual Sword that Affirms Truth through Mercy's Joy.

Now you might say, I want continue my journey down the same highway and want to still reach the destination at the end of the road but I don't want to have to work so hard to acquire and maintain the first list of equipment.

Well, unfortunately, you are in luck. Because there is a set of equipment that will take you to the end of the road with a lot of less effort. I strongly advise you to not use any of these items, however only you have the right to choose what you equip yourself with.

It Grants Us…

-A shaky Slothful Spiritual Shield which Ignores Truth through Death's Numbness.

-A shaky Physical Belt of Wrath which Denies Truth through Death's Numbness.

-A shaky Emotional Helmet of Gluttony which Refuses Truth through Death's Numbness.

-A shaky Mental Sandals of Greed which Dismisses Truth through Death's Numbness.

-A shaky Social Breastplate of Envy which Averts Truth through Death's Numbness.

-A shaky Intimate Lustful Sword which Affirms Lies through Death's Numbness.

At this point you might be saying, "well truth isn't always joyful and sometimes truth is numbingly boring". That might be true in a different situation, but in this situation the truth is very joyful due to Mercy. The truth we are specifically referring to is the truth of mercy.

"What we willfully praise we will become!"

PRAYERFULLY AVAILABLE: GRACE VS LOSS

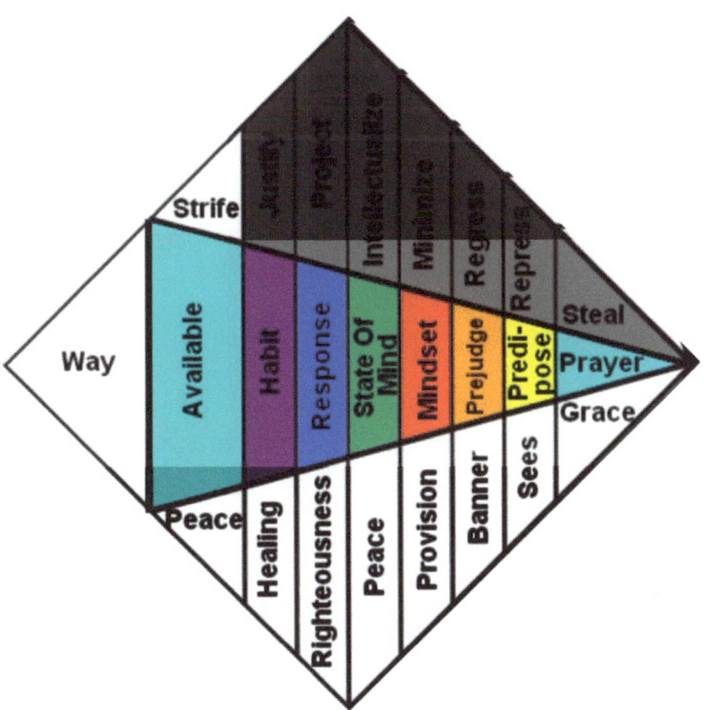

Now that we understand where we want to go and how we can get there, I think it's time to discuss what it takes to begin the journey!

Before we can arrive to our destination we must fight

through the trials and tribulations along the path that takes us to the end. Which we will only be victorious if we equip ourselves with the right equipment. However, before we can equip ourselves, we must first become strong enough to wear, hold, and use the equipment that we need.

Here is the list of things that we must obtain before we can equip ourselves with the means that will make the journey possible.

We Will Have…

-Strength of Sight beyond Spiritual Predisposition through Grace's Peace. (El Roi – God who Sees)

-Banner of Strength beyond Physical Prejudice through Grace's Peace. (Jehovah Nissi – God our Banner)

-Provisional Strength beyond Emotional Mindset through Grace's Peace. (Jehovah Jireh – God our Provider)

-Peaceful Strength beyond Mental State of Mind through Grace's Peace. (Jehovah Shalom – God our Peace)

-Strength of Righteousness beyond Social Response through Grace's Peace. (Jehovah Tsidkenu – God our Righteousness)

-Strength of Healing beyond Intimate Habits through Grace's Peace. (Jehovah Rapha – God our Healer)

As you can tell in the first list, it shows us that the God of Love gives us what we don't have in order to build us up to become something stronger then what we are without the God of Love. If the God of Love doesn't give us what we need then we are left with holes in each area of our life! However, when we don't go to the God of Love that doesn't mean we will be left with empty holes in our lives. Holes, no matter where they are or what they are made of will always accomplish their purpose.

Here is what the same holes become when they are filled with what the God of Fear has to offer.

We Will…

-Repress the Weakness of the Spiritual Predisposition through the Strife of Loss.

-Regress to the Weakness of the Physical Prejudice through the Strife of Loss.

-Minimize Weakness of the Emotional Mindset through the Strife of Loss.

-Intellectualize the Weakness of the Mental State of Mind through the Strife of Loss.

-Project Weakness of the Social Response through the Strife of Loss.

-Justify Weakness of the Intimate Habits through the Strife of Loss.

"To whom we pray determines who will answer!"

CONCLUSION

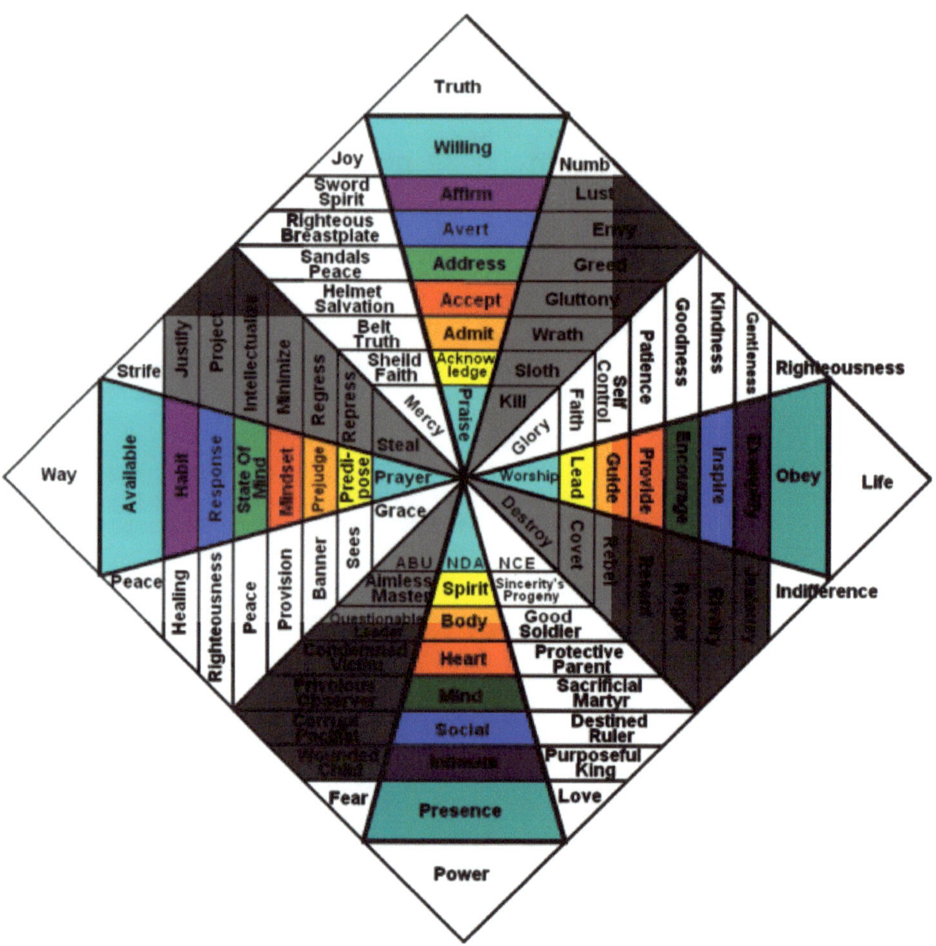

Below is a more extensive way to interpret the overall concepts in a more put together complete way.

POWER OF LOVE

Love's Progression in a Spiritual Journey - Becoming "Sincerity's Progeny"

When We Have…

Strength of Sight beyond Spiritual Predisposition through Grace's Peace.

It Grants Us…

A steady Spiritual Shield of Faith that Acknowledges Truth through Mercy's Joy.

Which Extends Our Reach to…

A perfectly balanced Faithful Spiritual Life when it's Lead by Glory's Righteousness.

Love's Progression in a Physical Journey – Becoming the "Good Soldier"

When We Have…

A Banner of Strength beyond Physical Prejudice through Grace's Peace.

It Grants Us…

A steady Physical Belt of Truth that Admits Truth through Mercy's Joy.

Which Extends Our Reach to…

A perfectly balanced Self-Controlled Physical Life when it's Guided by Glory's Righteousness.

Love's Progression in a Spiritual Journey – Becoming "Protective Parent"

When We Have…

Provisional Strength beyond Emotional Mindset through Grace's Peace.

It Grants Us…

A steady Emotional Helmet of Salvation that Accepts Truth through Mercy's Joy.

Which Extends Our Reach to…

A perfectly balanced Patient Emotional Life when it's Provided by Glory's Righteousness.

Love's Progression in a Spiritual Journey – Becoming "Sacrificial Martyr"

When We Have...

Peaceful Strength beyond the Mental State of Mind through Grace's Peace.

It Grants Us...

A steady Mental Sandals of Peace that Addresses Truth through Mercy's Joy.

Which Extends Our Reach to...

A perfectly balanced Good Mental Life when it's Encouraged by Glory's Righteousness.

Love's Progression in a Spiritual Journey – Becoming "Destined Ruler"

When We Have...

Strength of Righteousness beyond Social Response through Grace's Peace.

It Grants Us...

A steady Social Righteous Breastplate that Averts Lies through Mercy's Joy.

Which Extends Our Reach to...

A perfectly balanced Kind Social Life when it's Inspired by Glory's Righteousness.

Love's Progression in a Spiritual Journey – Becoming "Purposeful King"

When We Have...

Strength of Healing beyond Intimate Habits through Grace's Peace.

It Grants Us...

A steady Intimate Spiritual Sword that Affirms Truth through Mercy's Joy.

Which Extends Our Reach to...

A perfectly balanced Gentle Intimate Life when it's Exemplified by Glory's Righteousness.

POWER OF FEAR

Fear's Progression in a Spiritual Journey – Becoming "Aimless Master"

When We…

Repress Weakness as a Spiritual Predisposition through the Strife of Loss.

It Grants Us…

A shaky Slothful Spiritual Shield which Ignores Truth through Death's Numbness.

Which Limits Our Reach to…

A shifting Covetous Spiritual Life when it's Lead by Calamity's Indifference.

Fear's Progression in a Physical Journey – Becoming "Questionable Leader"

When We…

Regress to Weakness as a Physical Prejudice through the Strife of Loss.

It Grants Us…

A shaky Physical Belt of Wrath which Denies Truth through Death's Numbness.

Which Limits Our Reach to…

A shifting Rebellious Physical Life when it's Guided by Calamity's Indifference.

Fear's Progression in an Emotional Journey – Becoming "Condemned Victim"

When We…

Minimize Weakness as an Emotional Mindset through the Strife of Loss.

It Grants Us…

A shaky Emotional Helmet of Gluttony which Refuses Truth through Death's Numbness.

Which Limits Our Reach to…

A shifting Resentful Emotional Life when it's Provided by Calamity's Indifference.

Fear's Progression in a Mental Journey – Becoming "Frivolous Observer"

When We...

Intellectualize Weakness as a Mental State of Mind through the Strife of Loss.

It Grants Us...

A shaky Mental Sandals of Greed which Dismisses Truth through Death's Numbness.

Which Limits Our Reach to...

A shifting Regretful Mental Life when it's Encouraged by Calamity's Indifference.

Fear's Progression in a Social Journey – Becoming "Corrupt Pacifist"

When We...

Project Weakness as a Social Response through the Strife of Loss.

It Grants Us...

A shaky Social Breastplate of Envy which Averts Truth through Death's Numbness.

Which Limits Our Reach to...

A shifting Rivalrous Social Life when it's Inspired by Calamity's Indifference.

Fear's Progression in an Intimate Journey – Becoming "Wounded Child"

When We...

Justify Weakness of the Intimate Habits through the Strife of Loss.

It Grants Us...

A shaky Intimate Lustful Sword which Affirms Lies through Death's Numbness.

Which Limits Our Reach to...

A shifting Jealous Intimate Life when it's Inspired by Calamity's Indifference.

PROOF OF THE POWER OF 42!

Below is the equation that I prove that the Power of Love & Fear is the hands of 42!

3 Spiritual Questions + 3 answers + 1 *outcome = 7
3 Physical Questions + 3 answers + 1 *outcome = 7
3 Emotional Questions + 3 answers + 1 *outcome = 7
3 Mental Questions + 3 answers + 1 *outcome = 7
3 Social Questions + 3 answers + 1 *outcome = 7
3 Intimate Questions + 3 answers + 1 *outcome = 7

3 x 6 = 18 questions + 3 x 6 = 18 answers + 7 *outcomes = 42

(*outcome = "aimless master" or "Sincerity's Progeny")